BUSINESS SUCCESS

How To Incorporate Your Business

Peter Oliver

HOW TO INCORPORATE YOUR BUSINESSS
Copyright © 2016 by Concise Reads™

All rights reserved. No part of this book may be reproduced or transmitted in any form or by any means without written permission from the author.

DISCLAIMER: The author's books are only meant to provide the reader with the basic knowledge of a certain topic, without any warranties regarding whether the reader will, or will not, be able to incorporate and apply all the information provided. Although the author and publisher have made every effort to ensure that the information in this book was correct at press time, the author and publisher do not assume and hereby disclaim any liability to any party for any loss, damage, or disruption caused by errors or omissions, whether such errors or omissions result from negligence, accident, or any other cause.

CONCISE READS ™

Concise Reads was created to distill complex material into small morsels of knowledge that can be readily consumed by today's busy reader. At its core, Concise Reads is a living breathing brand that focuses on feeding knowledge to our always hungry entrepreneurial spirits. This knowledge is exactly what we wanted to learn but without having to pay thousands of dollars in fees for formal courses.

How much knowledge and how little time you spend to understand it, *together*, define value. We hope you enjoy the concise bits of value in the Concise Reads books, and we hope to continue to create more titles with time.

TABLE OF CONTENTS

Introduction ....
Why Did I Start This Business? ....
Choosing the Best Legal Structure ....
    Sole Proprietorship ....
    Partnerships..
    Limited Liability Companies..................
    Corporations ....
        S Corporation ....
        C Corporation................................
        Benefit Corporation.......................
How to Incorporate ....
    Best State to Incorporate In ....
    The DIY Approach ....
    Online Incorporation Services ....
    Working with a Small Business Lawyer.........
Final Thoughts ....

INTRODUCTION

Thinking of incorporating your business? Have questions about which business entity is right for you – limited liability company (LLC), S Corporation, partnership, or sole proprietor?

While many business owners realize the benefits of incorporation, they may feel the process is too daunting to tackle, but it does not need to be that way. Many small business owners remain sole proprietorships because they cannot answer the question, "How do I incorporate?". In fact, the most popular business entity by default is sole proprietorships. As we will learn later in the book, sole proprietorships work for some business but not others.

When incorporating, the information and questions concerning what to do and how to do it can be overwhelming and confusing. Learning the entire process of incorporation can be a lengthy process, which requires specific paperwork and forms to be filed depending on each unique scenario. In turn, incorrectly filed paperwork can prove detrimental to your business, not to mention detract from your day-to-day duties of running your own business.

Since incorporating is one of the biggest steps a business owner will take, it should be something that every business owner becomes familiar with and understands. This book aims to demystify the incorporation process by offering the major advantages and disadvantages to each entity formation. It is meant to be a guide to understanding the how and the why of business incorporation.

If you don't know anything about incorporation or liability or what is the right entity for a new or growing business, then it's time to pick up this concise reads and read it today.

WHY DID I START A COMPANY?

"If one does not know to which port one is sailing, no wind is favorable."
- Lucius Annaeus Seneca

Successful businesses require a lot of time, dedication, and effort. Undoubtedly, there is a reason behind your decision to strike out on your own as opposed to working in what others believe to be a safe steady paycheck job. You could also be forced to venture out on your own because of a downturn in the economy or in your employment.

To make the process of registering for a business license smoother, you have to start by answering the question 'Why did I start a company?' This is important. Were you working out of your garage and decided it was time for a more official storefront to attract customers? Was there a gap in the market that you could fill with your own contracting services? Did you feel that you could make a real difference in your neighborhood by establishing a business? Nailing down exactly why you started your company and getting a handle on how you envision the future of your business will help you discover the right business entity.

For example if you are a small business owner looking to separate the business's debts from your personal assets, without getting muddled down in tax and administrative obligations then a limited liability company

(LLC) is a great fit. Corporations, on the other hand, will have an easier time finding investors.

The next question you should ask yourself is: **Do I want to attract outside investment?**

It is possible to invest in an LLC, but many investors and firms prefer investing in a company that will eventually have an initial public offering since this will most likely give them a better return. You can sell stakes in an LLC, but any investor that buys a stake, even a small one, will usually have full management rights. So unlike a corporation, which can have stockholders that aren't involved in the day-to-day operations of a company, any investor in an LLC could be meddlesome. Corporations are therefore a better fit for entrepreneurs and business owners looking for outside investors.

However, this can open you up to legal action from shareholders if you're not succeeding at running the company.

This leads to the next question you want to ask yourself: **Will I need any extra protection?**

Forming a corporation means you have a financial duty to your stockholders. Every business decision must be made with a mind for maximizing profit. If you founded your company with the intent to make an impact along with a profit, your social mission might have to be abandoned. However, at the same time, there are also investors looking specifically to help businesses that are trying to make a positive impact. The movement towards investing in socially conscious companies has led to the formation of a new type of corporation, the **Benefit Corporation** (B-corp), which will be discusses later in the book.

While you can always change your business's structure later on, choosing and sticking with one particular structure will make life for your business easier as you continue building it. If you're not sure what entity best fits your business, this book was written to provide you with an overview of the pros and cons of the most popular structures which will help guide you in choosing the structure that best fits your needs both in the short-term and in the long-term.

Take some time to answer these 3 questions before moving on to the next section.

CHOOSING THE BEST LEGAL STRUCTURE

"If you want to have a strong structure, build the foundations the right way."
-Eraldo Banovac

Choosing the right business structure when starting a new business can be a confusing process and at times overwhelming. There are many business structures you could potentially choose: S corporations, C-corporations, professional corporation, nonprofit corporation, LLC, sole proprietorship, general partnership, and limited partnership.

When deciding the best structure for your business, use the following five factors to help guide your thought process:

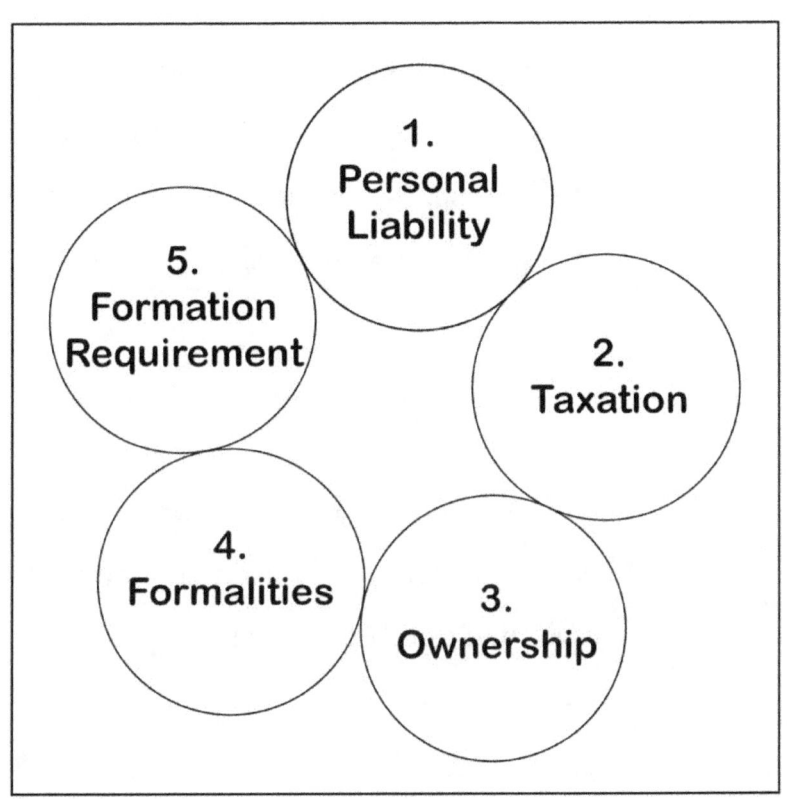

The questions to ask yourself are:

1. Do I need personal liability protection?

   _____

2. In terms of taxes, do I want to report my earnings on my own tax return or do I plan to split corporate profits among owners and the business?

   _____

3. Do I want to be the sole owner or do I have partners and need to have an unlimited number of owners?

   _____

4. Do I want to create the company simply and inexpensively, with minimal filing requirements or am I willing and able to write up articles of incorporation, by-laws, file various documents, obtain an employer identification number etc.?

_____

5. Am I prepared for substantial reporting responsibilities including annual reports, minutes, formal board meetings?

_____

Remember there is no one-size-fits-all approach. These questions are meant as a starting point on your journey to incorporation. Consider each question and use a checklist to determine which one best fits your own needs.

You'll finish this book wiser and better equipped to make a decision for your business, your family, your friends, or yourself.

Now let's get started.

Sole Proprietorships

Sole-proprietorship is the simplest form of doing business and is typically the default business structure entrepreneurs and small business owners wind up working with. While it's easy to form, it doesn't provide you with much legal protection. If your business doesn't take off quite like you expected, or if the business is sued, debtors could seize your personal assets to pay for the business's liabilities.

Now let's look at sole proprietorships based on our five factors.

1) **Personal Liability Protection:** None

2) **Taxation:** Your expenses and income from the business are included on your personal tax return. In other words, the business itself is not taxed separately. You report income and/or losses and expenses on Schedule C and the standard personal tax return, Form 1040. (The "bottom-line amount" from Schedule C transfers to your personal tax return.) It's your responsibility to withhold and pay all income taxes, including self-employment (of 15.3% on net income generated by your business) and estimated taxes.

3) **Ownership:** You own the company yourself or are self-employed.

4) **Formation Requirements:** You do not have to take any formal action to form a

sole proprietorship. In fact, as long as you are the only owner, this status automatically comes from your business activities. No Tax ID number (EIN) is required. No doing business as (DBA) registration is required. No business bank account is required, although for book-keeping purposes and audit protection one is recommend. In fact, you may already have formed one without knowing it. If you are a freelance writer, for example, you are a sole proprietor.

5) **Formalities:** None. No need to have annual meetings or keep meeting minutes.

+PROS: Any business losses you suffer may offset the income you have earned from your other sources. It's a low-cost and easy option, especially if you're looking to test your business concept. Additionally, because you are a sole owner, you have complete control.

What this means is that if your side business of teaching yoga on the weekend is losing money, you can deduct the loss from that business from your pre-tax income. Thus, you owe the government less money and your business loss is reduced.

-CONS: You are on the hook for all your company's liabilities. That means if your business seeks bankruptcy protection or you get sued, your personal assets may be at risk, and could be seized. If you are profitable, the self employment tax (which consists of social security and medicare taxes) kicks in. Additionally, sole proprietors often face challenges when trying to raise money. Because you can't sell stock in the business, investors won't invest if they can't get a piece of the pie. Banks are also hesitant to lend to a sole proprietorship because of a perceived lack of credibility when it comes to repayment if the business fails.

BEST FOR: Business owners with no or few employees, such as consultants, who can handle legal risk with adequate insurance or do not have assets to protect (i.e. just starting out in life).

Tip! Unless there is a major liability, partnership, or tax issue, starting out as a sole proprietorship is a great fit. Make sure your business is viable and don't worry about getting too complex too quickly.

Partnerships

There are two types of partnerships: general and limited. In a general partnership, a creditor may go after any or all of the partners. A limited partnership is comprised of a general partner with unlimited personal liability and limited partners whose liability is generally limited to the amount they have invested in the company. You have to report profits and losses in an <u>informational</u> tax return, and then file with your personal tax return.

1) **Personal Liability Protection:** In a <u>general</u> partnership, liability is divided equally among partners. A <u>limited</u> partnership allows partners to have limited liability, often based on the extent of each partner's investment percentage.

2) **Taxation:** You will need to register with the IRS, register with state and local revenue agencies, and obtain a tax ID number or permit.

A partnership must file an "annual information return" to report the income, deductions, gains and losses from the business's operations, but the business itself does not pay income tax. Instead, the business "passes through" any profits or losses to its partners. Partners include their respective share of the partnership's income or loss on their personal tax returns.

3) **Ownership:** Multiple partners or owners.

4) **Formation Requirements:** To form a partnership, you must register your business with your state, a process generally done through your Secretary of State's office. You'll also need to establish your business name. For partnerships, your legal name is the name given in your partnership agreement or the last names of the partners. If you choose to operate under a name different than the officially registered name, you will most likely have to file a fictitious name (also known as an assumed name, trade name, or DBA name, short for "doing business as").

5) **Formalities:** Partnerships must provide Schedule K-1 (Form 1065), which report each shareholder's share

of income, losses, deductions and credits, to all partners. (The shareholders use the information on the K-1 to report the same thing on their own separate tax returns.) Form 1065 is required to be filed, including extensions.

+PROS: It's another relatively low-cost and easy way to form a business. Plus, there usually can be some tax advantages to reporting your share of the profits and losses on your personal tax return.

-CONS: General partners can be personally at risk, even if another partner is the one who sinks the company. Make sure to choose wisely when it comes to picking responsible partners.

BEST FOR: Businesses that will be owned and operated by several individuals. It's a common structure in the real estate industry for example.

Limited Liability Companies

LLCs are fantastic entities that were created to provide the liability protection that corporations enjoy without the <u>double taxation</u>. Earnings and losses pass through to the owners and are included on their personal tax returns.

1) **Personal Liability Protection:** <u>Yes</u>.

2) **Taxation:** LLCs are subject to self-employment (SE) tax or 15.3% of net income generated from running of the business. The SE tax consists of Social Security and Medicare taxes. When you work most jobs, your earnings are taxed at a 6.2% rate for Social Security and

1.45% for Medicare. Additionally, your employer also contributes the same amount—a total of 7.65% of your wages. However, when you're self-employed, you are the employer and the employee. Therefore, you are responsible for paying all of the Social Security and Medicare taxes, which adds up to 15.3%.

Earnings and losses pass through to the owners and are included on their personal tax returns. Since the federal government does not recognize an LLC as a business entity for taxation purposes, all LLCs must file as a corporation, partnership, or sole proprietorship tax return. LLCs that are not automatically classified as a corporation can choose their business entity classification. The classification mainly affects what tax form you end up filing.

To elect a classification, an LLC must file Form 8832. This form is also used if an LLC wishes to change its classification status.

You should file the following tax forms depending on your classification:

- Single Member LLC. A single-member LLC files Form 1040 Schedule C like a sole proprietor.

- Partners in an LLC. Partners in an LLC file Form 1065, a partnership tax return, like owners in a traditional partnership.

- LLC filing as a Corporation. An LLC designated as a corporation files Form 1120, the corporation income tax return.

Combining the Benefits of an LLC with an S Corp

There is always the possibility of requesting S-Corp status (which limits SE tax) for your LLC. You'll have to make a special election with the IRS to have the LLC taxed as an S-Corp using Form 2553. You must file prior to the first two months and fifteen days of the beginning of the tax year in which the election is to take effect.

Tip! The best way to limit SE tax is to incorporate as an S corporation. However, one of the major benefits of an LLC is that you can obtain liability protection early on while your net income may still be low or inconsequential, but later convert to an S-Corp when the time is right.

3) **Ownership:** Member owned.

4) **Formation Requirements:** While each state has slight variations to forming an LLC, they all adhere to some general principles:

A. Choose a Business Name.

There are 3 rules that your LLC name needs to follow: (1) it must be different from an existing LLC in your state, (2) it must indicate that it's an LLC (such as "LLC" or Limited Company") and (3) it must not include words restricted by your state (such as "bank" and "insurance"). Your business name is automatically registered with your state when you register your business, so you do not have to go through a separate process.

Searching Available Names: Many state government websites have a business name search engine, however because many of them are not kept up to date, they might ask you to send a formal request or a 'Name Availability Inquiry Letter' that asks the state to check if the name you want is available. All the listed public company business names are available using the EDGAR search engine of the U.S. Securities and Exchange Commission. Most likely, your name will be unique enough. Other times you'll have to add a few extra characters.

The industry your business name is registered under is a 6-digit code known as the North American Industry Classification System (NAICS). This was released in 1997 to replace the older 4-digit code known as the Standard Industrial Classification (SIC). The SEC still uses the SIC for listing public companies.

B. File the Articles of Organization.

The "articles of organization" is a simple document that legitimizes your LLC and includes information like your business name, address, and the names of its members. For most states, you file with the Secretary of State. However, other states may require that you file with a different office such as the State Corporation Commission, Department of Commerce and Consumer Affairs, Department of Consumer and Regulatory Affairs, or the Division of Corporations & Commercial Code. Note: there may be an associated filing fee.

C. Create an Operating Agreement.

Most states do not require operating agreements. However, an operating agreement is highly recommended for multi-member LLCs because it structures your LLC's finances and organization, and provides rules and regulations for smooth operation. The operating agreement usually includes percentage of interests, allocation of profits and losses, member's rights and responsibilities and other provisions. The operating agreement is ultimately an internal document. If required, you'll submit it during incorporation. However, after you submit, you have the right to amend them as many times as you want and at any time.

D. Announce Your Business.

Some states, including Arizona and New York, require the extra step of publishing a statement in your local newspaper about your LLC formation. Check with your state's business filing office for requirements in your area.

5) **Formalities:** None

+PROS: LLCs offer liability protection without some of the formalities of a corporation, and tend to be less expensive to set up. This structure (unlike an S corporation, which we will discuss later) offers no limit on the number of shareholders it can have.

-CONS: Depending on how the entity elects to be taxed, you may have to pay self-employment tax on your share of the draw.

BEST FOR: This adaptable structure is popular among businesses that are just starting out and not totally sure how much they will grow in the first year or so. If you own rental property, you should consider an LLC. If you are in a partnership, need asset protection, and might want to convert to an S-Corp later on, consider an LLC.

Corporations

A corporation is an independent legal entity, separate from its owners, which means greater protection from personal liability in case the company is sued or files for bankruptcy. Along with shareholders, corporations are held accountable to a board of directors, which are elected by the shareholders. The board of directors meet to discuss and guide corporate affairs anywhere from once a month to once a year.

If the corporation is small, the shareholders should prepare and sign a shareholders buy-sell agreement. This contract provides that if a shareholder dies or wants to sell his or her stock, it must first be offered to the surviving shareholders. It also may provide for a method to determine the fair price that should be paid for those shares. Such agreements are usually funded with life insurance to purchase the stock of deceased shareholders.

If a corporation is large and sells its shares to many individuals, it may have to register with the Securities and Exchange Commission (SEC) or state regulatory bodies. More common is the corporation with only a few shareholders, which can issue its shares without any such registration under private offering exemptions.

Corporations file Form 1120 with the IRS and pay their own taxes. Salaries paid to shareholders who are employees of the corporation are deductible. But dividends paid to shareholders aren't deductible and therefore don't reduce the corporation's tax liability.

S Corporation

The S-Corporation is the most common. An S corporation (sometimes referred to as an S Corp) is a special type of corporation created through an IRS tax election. An eligible domestic corporation can avoid double taxation (once to the corporation and again to the shareholders) by electing to be treated as an S corporation.

An S Corp is a corporation with the Subchapter S designation from the IRS. To be considered an S Corp, you must first charter a business as a corporation in the state where it is headquartered. According to the IRS, S corporations are "considered by law to be a unique entity, separate and apart from those who own it." This limits the financial liability for which you (the owner, or "shareholder") are responsible.

What makes the S Corp different from a traditional corporation (C Corp) is that profits and losses can pass through to your personal tax return (Form 1040). Consequently, the business is not taxed itself. Only the shareholders are taxed.

There is an important caveat, however: any shareholder who works for the company must pay him or herself "reasonable compensation." For example, if you are running an ad agency and you want to pay yourself $30,000, but then find out that the average advertising professional earns $70,000 you will have a hard time making the case that $30,000 is reasonable compensation. Basically, the shareholder must be paid fair market value, or the IRS might reclassify any additional corporate earnings as wages. In our example an additional $40,000 of corporate earnings could be reclassified as employee compensation.

1) **Personal Liability Protection:** Yes.

2) **Taxation:** All states do not tax S Corps equally. Most recognize them similarly to the federal government and tax the shareholders accordingly.

However, some states (like Massachusetts) tax S Corps on profits above a specified limit. Other states don't recognize the S Corp election and treat the business as a C Corp with all of the tax ramifications. Some states (like New York and New Jersey) tax both the S Corps profits and the shareholder's proportional shares of the profits. You can see why state selection matters for S Corp tax purposes.

Your corporation must file the Form 2553 to elect "S" status within two months and 15 days after the beginning of the tax year or any time before the tax year for the status to be in effect.

3) **Ownership:** Shareholder owned.

4) **Formation Requirements:** To file as an S Corporation, you must first file as a corporation. After you are considered a corporation, all shareholders must sign and file Form 2553 to elect your corporation to become an S Corporation.

5) **Formalities:** None. No need to have annual meetings or keep meeting minutes.

Final Comments on S Corp:

As discussed earlier, there is always the possibility of requesting S Corp status for your LLC. You'll have to make a special election with the IRS to have the LLC taxed as an S Corp using Form 2553. And you must file it before the first two months and fifteen days of the beginning of the tax year in which the election is to take effect. The LLC remains a limited liability company from a legal standpoint, but for tax purposes it's treated as an S Corp.

An S Corp requires that you have no more than **100** shareholders (if you do, you will have to be taxed as a C Corp). It is also important to note that an S Corp cannot have a non-resident alien as a shareholder (important for young startups between friends of different nationalities), and cannot have more than one class of stock.

The idea behind having more than one class of stock is to give more rights to one class of stock versus another. Google and Facebook founders (C Corps) own the class of stock that has 10x shareholder voting rights, thus giving them more control of the company compared to the similar priced class of stock with only 1x voting rights.

The good news is that S Corps can have different classes of shares with different voting rights. The IRS only cares about the classes having "identical rights to distribution and liquidation proceeds" or have equal equity value of the company. Thus if an S Corp is a stepping stone towards a C Corp, you can elect to have different classes of stock to sell to investors, as long as they are different only in the matter of voting vs. non-voting rights.

C Corporation

C-corporations are mainly used to set up high-profile ventures. Almost every Fortune 500 company is a C-corp, and for specific reasons such as raising capital and conforming to securities laws in order to go public.

1) **Personal Liability Protection:** Yes.

2) **Taxation:** C Corps are separate taxable entities. They file a corporate tax return (Form 1120) and pay taxes at the corporate level. There is a separate tax rate schedule for corporations, with rates ranging from 15 percent to 35 percent.

   C Corps face the possibility of double taxation if corporate income is distributed to business owners as dividends, which are considered personal income. Tax on corporate income is paid first at the corporate level and again at the individual level on dividends.

3) **Ownership:** Shareholder owned. Unlike an SCorp there are no limitations on the number of shareholders.

4) **Formation Requirements:** Formation documents must be filed with the state. These documents, typically called the Articles of Incorporation or Certificate of Incorporation. Furthermore, to operate a corporation, there must be by-laws, or governing rules for the corporation. For example, the business year for the corporation, the compensation for the officers, time and

place for meetings of officers, shareholders and directors. State law may outline many required rules; corporations can in some cases create their own rules.

5) **Formalities:** C corporations are required to adhere to certain regulations to protect the company's corporate status. They must hold at least one meeting per year for shareholders and directors. The minutes from shareholder and director meetings must be kept to demonstrate how the company makes its decisions. A C corporation's minutes will include a voting record for the company's shareholders and directors. A corporate ledger should be maintained to list the name and ownership percentage of each shareholder. C corporations are required to file annual reports and financial

statements with each state where the company conducts business. Written bylaws that state the rules and regulations of the company must be kept at the C corporation's primary business location.

Tip! The C-Corp was primarily designed for and is used by public companies to raise capital with thousands, if not millions, of shareholders. However, for the average small-business owner or startup, all this is unnecessary.

+PROS: Corporate debt is not considered that of its owners therefore you do not necessarily risk your personal assets, beyond your investment in the corporation.

-CONS: It is more expensive and complex, requiring more accounting and tax preparation help to ensure you are following all the rules especially filing the correct documents.

BEST FOR: Businesses that need liability protection and flexibility to grow into a large organization. It is a common structure for manufacturers and restaurant chains.

Benefit Corporation

There's a new type of corporation, the Benefit Corp or "Benefit Corporation" that allows you to mix social impact with shareholder demands. If you want to build a company with a mission that's bigger than just earning a profit, a Benefit Corp allows you to act on your social or environmental mission without having to cave to your shareholders.

While a company classified as a Benefit Corp is still described as a for-profit company and therefore must still act in the interest of its shareholders, there's a caveat: Benefit Corps are not judged solely on financial performance but also on its impact on the world around it.

Want to start an initiative with your company for improving the town your business is based in? You can do this without fear from your shareholders if you're classified as a Benefit Corp. As a Benefit Corp, you have the right to set aside a specific amount of profits that you'd like to use for public benefit, such as charities. Furthermore, when you go to sell your company, you're not obligated to sell it to the highest bidder either, which allows you to take other factors into account during the sales process.

As of the writing of this book, 31 states recognize the B Corp as a business classification:

Arizona	Colorado	Florida	Illinois
Arkansas	Connecticut	Hawaii	Indiana
California	Delaware	Idaho	Louisiana

Maryland	New Hampshire	Rhode Island	Virginia
Massachusetts		South Carolina	Washington DC
Minnesota	New Jersey		West Virginia
Montana	New York	Tennessee	
Nebraska	Oregon	Utah	
Nevada	Pennsylvania	Vermont	

7 additional states have pending legislation and are on track to recognize the B Corp in the near future:

Alaska	Iowa	Michigan	Oklahoma
Georgia	Kentucky	Ohio	

1) **Personal Liability Protection:** Yes.

2) **Taxation:** There are no additional tax benefits from being a B Corp. In fact, a

B Corp company must elect to be taxed as a C or S corp.

3) **Ownership**: Shareholders.

4) **Formation Requirements:** When a company applies for a B Corp status, it has to take a rigorous test—The Impact Assessment test—with an unbiased governing body called the B Lab. The test has more than 200 points that evaluate different issues and aspects of your business, and you'll have to score 80% or higher to pass. If a company passes the test, it will be held to incredibly strict practices and policies.

5) **Formalities:** B Corps are required to make available to the public, except in Delaware, an annual benefit report that

assesses their overall social and environmental performance against a third party standard.

+PROS: Directors are legally protected to make decisions based on non-financial goals, and those goals are protected through times of transition.

-CONS: Additional administrative burden because Benefit Corps require that your company's impact be documented and verifiable.

INCORPORATING

You know you have to incorporate. What you're not sure is exactly how to do it without investing a great deal of time and money.

Perhaps the main advantage to incorporating is that it limits your personal liability for negligence or breach of contract. If your business is incorporated and you maintain the documentation and separation of personal and corporate finances as you should, then you may significantly reduce your personal financial risk if you are sued for breach of contract or some other liability. Before we go into how to incorporate let's first talk about where to incorporate.

Best State to Incorporate In

If you have been researching corporations or LLCs, you've surely heard that forming your entity in states like Delaware, Nevada and Wyoming can offer you various benefits above and beyond what your state can offer you. While it may be true that these states do have some benefits, you have to consider whether or not those benefits even apply to you. I.e. Does it even matter where you incorporate?

Whenever a corporation or LLC transacts business in a particular state, <u>it must register</u> with that state. This means that it has to pay taxes in that state and file reports, just as if it was actually formed there.

If you are operating a "local" business that caters to customers that mainly live in the state you reside in, it generally would not make sense for you to form your corporation or LLC in a different state only to then need to register in your home state anyway.

For example, if you do business in New York, you will need to register your company there anyway and pay the necessary state taxes. In fact, if you don't take the time to register your entity in the sate where you are operating the business, you will be personally exposed and have no protection at all. By incorporating in Delaware, all you do is increase your administrative costs and create headaches with additional state fillings. While there are exceptions, in most cases, you might as well just form your entity in the state in which you live and keep things easy on yourself! Why have the extra fees, taxes and paperwork?

Tip! A good way to determine whether or not you are "transacting business" in your home state is if you lease office space or have employees there. If either of these are the case, then you will most likely be required to register to transact business in your state and it will be much easier if you just form your corporation or LLC there in the first place.

If you do not have a brick and mortar business, such as an internet-based company or a consulting business, then you may have some more options open to you. Since Corporations and LLCs are entities entirely separate from you

– they are like separate people – which means that they can live wherever they choose, which may or may not be the same state that you live in.

Some states have more favorable tax laws or better corporate infrastructures. This means that the laws are more corporate friendly and it is easier to file paperwork in that state. That's why many large internet companies have incorporated in Delaware. On the other hand, if income tax is more of a concern, Wyoming, Nevada, South Dakota, and Texas have no corporate taxes.

If you have spoken to your attorney and have determined that your business is in fact not transacting business in your state, then you have a decision to make!

Tip! Are there more advantages in some states? Yes, if you are doing business in that state! For most businesses, you should incorporate in the state in which you conduct business.

Now that we have discussed where to incorporate, here's what you need to know about the simplest, easiest (and cheapest) ways to incorporate your new business, from least expensive to most expensive.

The DIY Approach to Incorporation

This method has the advantage of being the least expensive, but it also requires you to personally do the most work. You will have to:

- Choose which state you want to incorporate in
- Create and register a business name with that state
- As discussed in the prior chapter, determine for yourself which type of corporation you want your business to be
- Register with the Internal Revenue Service as well as state and local revenue agencies in order to obtain a tax ID

(Form SS-4) and all necessary permits and licenses
- Complete the articles of incorporation documents yourself and file them with your state's Secretary of State Office
- Prepare your corporate bylaws, record minutes from your first Board of Directors' meeting, and issue stock yourself

Because each state has its own requirements you will have to inquire with your state (usually the "Division of Corporation") to determine the exact Forms to file and fees to pay.

Online Incorporation Services

Incorporation services (such as legalzoom and rocketlawyer) are able to explain the different types of corporations (such as LLCs, S-corporations, and C-corporations) to help you determine the best type of incorporation for your needs. These services generally offer affordable packages of services for small or mid-sized businesses to help them incorporate. Costs range from under $100 to near $1,000. Services performed by incorporation services include:

- Name availability search

- Preparation and filing of formation documents

- Preparation and filing of your Tax ID number

- Obtaining certified copies of state-filed documents
- Creating LLC Announcements and certificates of publication

- Preparing and filing state sales tax applications

Working with a Small Business Lawyer

Hiring a start-up or small business lawyer is the traditional method of incorporation, and it usually costs more than using an incorporation service. Your small business lawyer will register your business name, ensure that you have all necessary permits, and generally keep you on the right side of the law.

An advantage of incorporating with the help of a small business attorney would be his or her expertise about the law and your risks if your business is in a high-profile or high-risk industry.

With businesses that have multiple founders, hiring a small business lawyer for incorporating is a good way of making sure that each of the founders has the appropriate agreements between himself or herself and the corporation. These partner agreements, when professionally written, could save you a few headaches down the road if there is disagreement among the partners.

If you are also looking to raise money, then you should seek information and advice from a lawyer since this can be a complex process and when you are looking to get investors you want to have established your company correctly.

Overall, whether you choose to incorporate your self or seek out professional help, the process should not be too difficult or time-consuming. However, you want to make sure that you are choosing the best options for your company.

Recommendations

Once you've determined that incorporation would benefit your business, using an incorporation service is something you should strongly consider. You will save money over the cost of hiring a small business lawyer, and you save time over doing the incorporation yourself. For a large number of business owners, however, using an incorporation service provides the best combination of affordability and simplicity, so if you're considering incorporating, you should start by first visiting the website of these incorporation services and see if they're a good choice for you.

Of course, there are exceptions. Someone with a business in an industry where liability can be high or where partner agreements or operating agreements will likely be complex will probably find the greatest peace of mind by working with a small business lawyer, particularly one who is experienced in that industry.

On the other hand, a business owner with a legal background may not find the do-it-yourself approach to be overwhelming at all and simply going through the process of incorporation is a great lesson that better prepares you to submit future documents yourself.

FINAL THOUGHTS

Incorporating a business provides many benefits, including limiting your personal liability and making your business easier to transfer to others. Limiting your personal assets will protect your home and other belongings from being seized as collateral. Put another way, if your corporation cannot pay its bills, the creditors can only recover from the assets of your company. Sole proprietors and general partners in a partnership are personally liable for all debts and obligations of the business. This includes loans, accounts payable, judgments resulting from litigation, and business losses. Being incorporated enables you to:

- Legitimize the business.

- Limit your personal liability.
- Take your company public.
- Issue stock options to employees.
- Transfer ownership or shares among members of the corporation.
- Have your corporation outlive you.
- Raise investment capital.

Incorporating also makes it easier to raise funds for the business from outside investors. Issuing stock to be purchased by investors is more advantageous than taking out a bank loan and making interest payments especially if future short-term revenue is uncertain. The same can be said for corporate bonds.

Forming a corporation also provides numerous tax benefits. Corporations are taxed at a lower rate than individuals. Both regular corporations and LLCs may deduct normal business expenses like employee salaries before they allocate income to owners. Corporations can also deduct 100 percent of medical insurance premiums. Because corporations are separate legal entities, they can own shares in another corporation and receive corporate dividends 80 percent tax-free.

Some other benefits of incorporating include name protection and the sense of image that comes with it. Most states will not let another business file articles of incorporation with your exact name. This reduces confusion and helps you establish your brand. It also adds credibility and permanence. Having "Inc." or "LLC" after your business name adds instant authority. Consumers, vendors, and partners may prefer to do business with an incorporated company.

Finally, there is perpetuity. Permanence results from incorporating—whether you start with one person or several. As long as the owners comply with federal and state regulations, and keep filings up-to-date, a corporation exists forever. It survives the death of owners and shareholders.

The only way to end a corporation is through dissolution.

Appendix: Mentioned Tax Forms

- **Schedule K-1 Form 1065**: filed by each partner along with their personal income taxes.
- **Form 8832**: Used to elect entity classification for LLC
- **Form 2553**: Used to specifically elect S-corp classification for LLC.
- **1040**: Individual Tax Return
- **Schedule C**: Tax form filed in addition to personal tax forms (1040) by sole proprietorships and single-member LLCs
- **Schedule E**: Tax form filed in addition to personal tax form (1040) if you have a rental income
- **1065**: Tax form filed in addition to personal tax forms in a partnership LLC.
- **1120**: Tax form filed in addition to personal tax forms in an LLC classified

as a corporation. This is the company's income tax return.

- **SS-4**: IRS form to obtain tax ID

Be sure to check our other titles for a quick knowledge morsel.

Be sure to check our other titles for a quick knowledge morsel.

www.ingramcontent.com/pod-product-compliance
Lightning Source LLC
Chambersburg PA
CBHW070329190526
45169CB00005B/1818